BEST.
DAD JOKES.
EVER.

CHANTELLE GRACE

BroadStreet
PUBLISHING

BroadStreet Kids
Racine, Wisconsin, USA

BroadStreet Kids is an imprint of BroadStreet Publishing Group, LLC.
Broadstreetpublishing.com

BEST. DAD JOKES. EVER.

© 2018 by BroadStreet Publishing®

ISBN 978-1-4245-5645-8

Content compiled by Chantelle Grace.

Design by Chris Garborg | garborgdesign.com
Editorial services by Michelle Winger | literallyprecise.com

Printed in the United States of America.

18   19   20   21   22   23   7   6   5   4   3   2   1

Author Bio

CHANTELLE GRACE is a witty wordsmith who
loves music, art, and competitive games. She
is fascinated by God's intricate design of the
human body. As she works her way through
medical school, she knows it's important to
share the gift of laughter with those around
her. When she's not studying abroad, she
makes her home in Prior Lake, Minnesota.

TABLE OF CONTENTS .....

MY DAD SAID...

I asked my dad if I could go
to a 50-cent concert.

He gave me a dollar and said,

"Take your brother, too."

My dad didn't have 19 candles
for my last birthday,
but he had the number four. He put that
on the cake and said,

"It's 4 your birthday."

My dad always told me that the shovel...

was a ground-breaking invention.

When my dad drives past a cow pasture, he always says,

"That cow is out-standing in his field!"

Dad always tells me to avoid the sushi.

He says it's a little fishy.

My dad said they just made round bales of hay illegal on farms...

because cows weren't getting a square meal.

My dad said to a struggling singer,
"Don't forget a bucket.

You'll need it to carry a tune."

Every time I hurt myself, my dad says,

"It'll get better when it stops hurting."

I was sailing with my dad one afternoon.
He picked up a vegetable and said,

"Look, there's a leek in my boat!"

Every time I pulled out the Play-Doh
when I was young,
my dad would say,

"We're going to have doh much fun!"

My dad always told me,

"You can pick your friends,

and you can pick your nose,

but you can't pick your friend's nose."

My dad says bees have sticky hair...

because they use honey combs.

When I told my Dad that my pony
was hurt,

*he told me to take it
to the horse-pital.*

When I asked my dad if he had
any old batteries,

*he said he gave all the dead ones away
free of charge.*

My dad came to tell me that a red ship
and blue ship had crashed.

*He said apparently the crew
was marooned.*

My dad said if I want to start and run
a company,

that's my own business.

Whenever I was going out fishing,
my dad would say,

"Let minnow when you get there."

Whenever my dad puts the car in reverse,
he says,

"Ah, this takes me back."

When things weren't going great for me,
my dad would say,

"Cheer up! It could be worse.

You could be stuck underground in a hole
full of water."

I know he meant well.

When my dad orders a Cobb salad,
he always points to the chicken and the
egg and says,

"Which should I eat first?"

Whenever we drive over a railroad crossing, my dad says,

"A train has been here recently.

I can tell because there are tracks."

My dad took my headphones,

connected them to an empty soda bottle,

and told me he was listening to pop music.

My dad always told me that the leading cause of dry skin...

is towels.

DAD'S FAVORITE PUNS

I remember the first time I saw
a universal remote.

I thought,

Wow, this changes everything.

A sandwich walks into a smoothie shop
and orders a drink.

The cashier says,

*"We don't serve
food here."*

I only know 25 letters of the alphabet.

I don't know Y.

I had a dream I was a muffler last night.

I woke up exhausted.

FedEx and UPS are merging.

They're going to be Fed-Up from now on.

Two guys walk into a restaurant.

The third one goes through the door.

I decided to sell the duster and pan.

It was just collecting dust.

Two goldfish are in a tank.
One says to the other,

"Do you know how to drive this thing?"

I was interrogated over a stolen cheese toastie.

They really grilled me.

I thought about going on an almond-only diet,

but that's just nuts.

A steak pun is...

a medium rare well done.

I've never been on a gun range before.

I'd like to give it a shot.

3/2 people admit...

they're bad with fractions.

I cut my finger slicing cheese.

I think I have grater problems.

The cat is sick.

I don't think it's feline well.

I dreamed about drinking an entire ocean of orange soda.

It took a while for me to realize it was a Fanta sea.

I couldn't figure out my seatbelt.

Then it clicked.

I keep trying to lose weight.

It keeps finding me.

I'm terrified of elevators.

I'm going to take steps to avoid them.

RIP boiled water.

You will be mist.

Today a vegetarian said she saw me on the bus last week,

but I'd never seen herbivore.

I used to hate facial hair,

but then it grew on me.

I'd like to say thanks to all the sidewalks...

for keeping me off the street.

I was addicted to the hokey pokey,

but I turned myself around.

I got hit with a can of soda today.

It didn't hurt because it's a soft drink.

I'm like the fabric version of King Midas.

Everything I touch becomes felt.

I just realized 50% of Asia...

is A.

3.14% of sailors...

are pi-rates.

I just ate a frozen pear.

Hardcore.

I donut understand puns...

about desserts.

Singing in the shower is all fun and games until you get shampoo in your mouth.

Then it's a soap opera.

I used to be indecisive,

but now I'm not quite sure.

The advantages of origami...

are twofold.

I always used to get small shocks when touching metal objects.

Recently it stopped.

Needless to say, I'm ex-static.

My eye puns...

couldn't be cornea.

I'm afraid for the calendar.

Its days are numbered.

Did you hear about the circus fire?

It was in-tents.

My first elevator experience...

was so uplifting.

You know what they say about cliffhangers...

CROWD SOURCE

Dad: What do you call a man with a rubber toe?

Roberto.

Dad: Why did the invisible man turn down a job offer?

He couldn't see himself doing it.

Dad: What is Beethoven's favorite fruit?

A ba-na-na-na.

Dad: What do prisoners use
to call each other?

Cell phones.

Dad: Have you ever heard of a music
group called Cellophane?

They mostly wrap.

Dad: Did you hear about the guy who
invented knock-knock jokes?

He won the no-bell prize.

Dad: My friend David lost his ID.

Now I just call him Dav.

Dad: What do you call an elderly person with really good hearing?

Deaf defying.

Dad: I was trying to buy one of those checkout dividers,

but the silly cashier kept putting it back.

Dad: Have you met my friend Annette?

She's married to a fisherman.

Dad: Why did the redhead go to the dentist?

Ginger-vitis.

Dad: I asked a Frenchman if he played video games.

He said, "Wii."

Dad: Why do accountants always look good in heels?

Because they never lose their balance.

Dad: My friend ate a bunch of plastic horses.

It's okay. The doctors said his condition is stable.

Dad: Why did Santa's helper feel sad?

He had low elf esteem.

Dad: My doctor's chart said my blood type was A.

But it was a type O.

Dad: What did the police atom say to the suspect atom?

I've got my ion you.

Dad: What do you call an unpredictable, out of control photographer?

A loose Canon.

Dad: Did you hear about the sensitive burglar?

He takes things personally.

JUST A GAME

Dad: What did the mountain climber call his son?

Cliff.

Dad: I don't play soccer because I like the sport.

It's just for the kicks.

Dad: Why do scuba divers fall backward into the water?

Because if they fell forward they'd still be in the boat.

Dad: What time do tennis players love to play most?

Tennish.

Dad: I met your mother on the net.

We were both acrobats.

Dad: I love rowing.

It's oarsome.

Dad: I just played my first round of golf.
I'm not very good.

In fact, I've got a fairway to go.

Dad: Sometimes I squat on the floor,
put my arms around my legs,
and lean forward.

That's how I roll.

Dad: I used to have a fear of hurdles,

but I got over it.

Dad: If I refuse to go to the gym,

does that count as resistance training?

Dad: The depressing thing about tennis is that no matter how good I get,

I'll never be as good as the wall.

Dad: Why was the baseball player a bad sport?

He stole third base and then went home.

Dad: I'm taking part in a stair climbing competition.

Guess I better step up my game.

Dad: What do you call the heavy breathing someone makes while trying to hold a yoga pose?

Yoga pants.

A FEAST OF FUNNIES

Dad: A jumper cable walks into a restaurant.

The waitress says,

"I'll serve you, but don't start anything."

Dad: Did you know that milk is the fastest liquid on the planet?

It's pasteurized before you even see it.

Dad: Do you want to hear my pizza joke?

Never mind, it's too cheesy.

Dad: Why did the coffee file a police report?

It got mugged.

Dad: What does an angry pepper do?

It gets jalapeño face.

Dad: What do you call a lonely cheese?

Provolone.

Dad: How many apples grow on a tree?

All of them.

Dad: Did you know French fries weren't actually cooked in France?

They were cooked in Greece.

Dad: Did you hear about the restaurant on the moon?

Great food, no atmosphere.

Dad: Did you hear about the angry pancake?

It just flipped.

Dad: When I went to a seafood disco last night,

I pulled a mussel.

Dad: Why did the girl smear peanut butter on the road?

To go with the traffic jam.

Dad: I'm on a seafood diet.

I see food and I eat it.

Dad: Do you know where you can get soup in bulk?

The soupermarket.

Dad: What do you call a can of soup that eats other cans of soup?

A Can-nibal.

Dad: You heard the rumor going around about butter?

Never mind, I shouldn't spread it.

Dad: Are you cooking out this weekend? Don't forget the pickle.

It's kind of a big dill.

Dad: You can't plant a vegetable garden...

if you haven't botany seeds.

Dad: Did you hear about the cheese factory in France?

It burned down and there was nothing left but de Brie.

Dad: Whenever I want to start eating healthy,

a chocolate bar looks at me and Snickers.

Dad: I burnt my Hawaiian pizza last night.

I should've put it on aloha setting.

Dad: I don't fear condiments on my food.

I relish it.

Dad: I've eaten too much Middle Eastern food.

Now I falafel.

Dad: I woke up with a face full of rice.

I must've fallen asleep as soon as my head hit the pilau.

Dad: The café messed up my coffee order,

but they gave me a new one.

Thanks a latte.

Dad: It's National Pancake Day!

That really creped up on us.

Dad: What happens when you tell an egg a joke?

It cracks up.

Dad: What did Ernie say when Bert asked if he wanted ice cream?

Surebert.

IN THE FAMILY

Dad: Last night, Mom and I watched three movies back-to-back.

Thankfully, I was the one facing the TV.

Dad: Did I tell you about the time I fell in love while doing a backflip?

I was heels over head.

Dad: Mom's water just broke.

I guess the baby finally ran out of womb.

Dad: How much does a teenager weigh?

An Instagram.

Dad: My wife told me I was average.

I think she's mean.

Dad: The invisible man married an invisible woman.

Their kids weren't really anything to look at.

Dad: My wife is on a tropical food diet; the house is full of the stuff.

It's enough to make a mango crazy.

Dad: My wife asked me to sync her phone,

so I threw it into the ocean.

Dad: After dinner my wife asked me if I could clear the table.

I needed a run up, but I made it.

Dad: My wife keeps telling me to stop pretending to be butter,

but I'm on a roll.

Dad: Don't kiss your wife with a runny nose.

You might think it's funny,

but it's snot.

Dad: I told my wife she drew her eyebrows too high.

She seemed surprised.

Mom: Do you want to go to yoga class with me?

Dad: Namaste here.

Dad: It's difficult to say what my wife does.

She sells seashells on the seashore.

Dad: My wife said she wanted something with diamonds for Christmas.

I got her a deck of cards.

Dad: My son opened the fridge last night, and threw a block of cheese at me. I said,

"That's really mature."

Mom: (Rubbing her stomach) I wonder if it's hot in there for the baby.

Dad: *It's likely womb-temperature.*

Mom: What do you think of our new couch?

Dad: *Sofa so good.*

ALL ABOUT ANIMALS

Dad: What would you call two spiders that just got married?

Newly-webs.

Dad: Why do you never see rhinos hiding in trees?

Because they're really good at it.

Dad: What do you call an elephant that isn't important?

Never mind. It's irrelephant.

Dad: What did the dad spider say to the kid?

"You're on the web too much."

Dad: What did the horse say after he tripped?

"Help, I've fallen and I can't giddy-up."

Dad: On what side do chickens have the most feathers?

The outside.

Dad: What do you call a cow with two legs?

Lean beef.

Dad: What about a cow with no legs?

Ground beef.

Dad: What do you call a fish with two knees?

A two-knee fish.

Dad: Why do chicken coops only have two doors?

If they had four, they would be called chicken sedans.

Dad: How do you take a sick pig to the hospital?

In a ham-bulance.

Dad: What is the loudest pet you can get?

A trumpet.

Dad: Where does a peacock go when it loses its tail?

A retail store.

Dad: What did the lion king say to Simba when he was walking too slowly?

"Mufasa."

Dad: Why do bees hum?

Because they don't know the words.

Dad: What do you call a group of killer whales that play instruments?

An orca-stra.

Dad: Why did the octopus beat the shark in a fight?

Because it was well armed.

Dad: A duck walks into a pharmacy and says,

"Give me some chap-stick. You can just put it on my bill."

Dad: What kind of fish is made of only two sodium atoms?

2 Na.

Dad: What do you call a cow that just had a baby?

A new moother.

Dad: Why do crabs never give to charities?

Because they're shellfish.

Dad: What's a duck's favorite dip?

Quackamole.

Dad: Your pet tortoises keep fighting.

It's a turtle disaster.

Dad: What did the dog say after a long day at work?

"Today was ruff."

Dad: Just read a few facts about frogs and toads.

They were ribbiting.

Dad: When a bear writes a contract,

beware the hidden claws.

Dad: Why do bears have hairy coats?

Fur protection.

Dad: The dog used to chase people on a bike a lot.

I had to take his bike away from him.

Dad: What did the hippo say when another hippo called him fat?

"That's very hippo-critical."

Dad: What do you call a dinosaur that knows lots of words?

A thesaurus.

Dad: Which horse is the most mysterious?

Black Beauty. He's a dark horse.

Dad: What did the Mexican say to his chicken?

"Oh-lay."

Dad: A pet shop was robbed last week.

There are currently no leads.

Dad: I ate some bad chicken last night.

Now I feel fowl.

Dad: I took the shell off my snail to make it faster,

but it became sluggish.

Dad: What did one bird say to the cheating parrot?

"Toucan play at that game."

Dad: What do you call a fly with no wings or legs?

A lie.

Dad: Why do cows have hooves instead of feet?

Because they lactose.

Dad: What do you call a lazy kangaroo?

A pouch potato.

Dad: What kind of corsage do you give a collie?

A collie flower.

Dad: A big cat escaped its cage at the zoo yesterday.

If I saw that, I'd puma pants.

Dad: How do hens cheer for their team?

They egg them on.

Dad: What happened to the dog that swallowed a firefly?

It barked with de-light.

Dad: What do you call bears with no ears?

B's.

Dad: What kind of dogs like car racing?

Lap dogs.

Dad: How do snails fight?

They slug it out.

Dad: What kind of bird sticks to sweaters?

A Vel-Crow.

Dad: What do you get when you cross a fish and an elephant?

Swimming trunks.

Dad: Why aren't koalas actual bears?

They don't meet the koalafications.

NATURAL DISASTER

Dad: What did one volcano say to the other?

"I lava you."

Dad: What do you use to cut an ocean in two?

A sea-saw.

Dad: What did one snowman say to the other?

"Do you smell carrots?"

Dad: What do clouds wear under their jeans?

Thunderpants.

Dad: Why was the big cat disqualified from the race?

Because it was a cheetah.

Dad: My seasickness...

comes in waves.

Dad: What lies at the bottom of the ocean and twitches?

A nervous wreck.

Dad: Is it just me, or are trees somewhat suspicious on sunny days?

They seem shady.

Dad: Did you see the movie about trees falling in love?

It's a bit sappy for me.

Dad: What did the beach say as the tide came in?

Long time no sea.

Dad: Mountains aren't just funny...

they're hill areas.

Dad: What did the planet say after the earthquake?

"Sorry, that was my fault. I'm very shook up about it."

Dad: What does a house wear?

Address.

Dad: When I was young, my friends talked me into jumping into the ocean.

It was pier pressure.

RIDDLE ME THIS

Dad: You're American when you go into the bathroom,

but what are you while you're in the bathroom?

European.

Dad: You're American when you go into the bathroom,

but what are you when you come out?

You're Finnish.

Dad: I have no body and no nose. Who am I?

Nobody knows.

Dad: I have six eyes, two mouths, and three ears. What am I?

Ugly.

Dad: If you see someone take an iPhone,

does that make you an iWitness?

Dad: Can February March?

No, but April May.

Dad: I am a factory that sells average products. What am I?

A satis-factory!

Dad: What's the difference between a hippo and a zippo?

One is really heavy and the other is a little lighter.

Dad: If a prisoner could take his own mug shot,

would it be called a cellfie?

Dad: What's the difference between a nicely dressed man on a bicycle and a poorly dressed man on a tricycle?

Attire.

Dad: How do you tell the difference between a crocodile and an alligator?

You will see one later and one in a while.

AT WORK

My dad used to work in a shoe recycling shop.

It was sole destroying.

My dad wants a job in the moisturizer industry.

He applies daily.

My dad just quit his job at Starbucks.

Day after day it was the same old grind.

My dad used to be a can-crusher.

He quit because it was soda-pressing.

My dad was at a job interview and got asked about a gap in his resumé.

He said he obviously fell asleep on his spacebar.

Dad used to have a job collecting leaves.

He was raking it in.

My dad is an archaeologist.

His career is in ruins.

My dad is a clock maker.

His job is very time consuming.

My dad was a comedian.
He told one too many light bulb jokes.

Then he burnt out.

My dad is an astronomer.
He got tired of watching the moon go around the earth for 24 hours.

He decided to call it a day and head home.

My dad got fired from the helium factory.

His boss didn't like the tone of his voice.

My dad lost his job last week.

Unemployment is not working for him.

My dad is a banker.

When he came home from work today,

he was worried about his job.

He said it's in the balance.

My dad is the lion's hairdresser at the zoo.

He's literally the mane man.

Everyone laughed when my dad said he was going to be a comedian.

They're not laughing now.

My dad is a chemist.

Periodically he like jokes about elements.

BACK TO SCHOOL

Dad: I'm reading a history book about glue.

I can't put it down. The information has really stuck with me.

Dad: The difference between a numerator and a denominator is a short line.

Only a fraction of people will understand this.

Dad: I hate perforated lines.

They're tear-able.

Dad: My kid wants to invent a pencil with an eraser on each end.

I just don't see the point.

Dad: I went out with a girl called Simile.

I don't know what I met-a-phor.

Dad: What's the worst thing about ancient history class?

The teachers tend to Babylon.

Dad: Do you want to hear a word I just made up?

Plagiarism.

Dad: I find whiteboards pretty great.

Actually, they are remarkable.

Dad: Dot-to-dots aren't always addictive.

You just have to know where to draw the line.

Dad: I will stop at nothing...

to avoid negative numbers.

Dad: I wish I was 23 again,

so I could be physically and mathematically in my prime.

I asked my dad to help me with a math problem.

He said, "Don't worry; this is a piece of cake."

I said, "No, it's a math problem."

He said, "Maybe it's pi?"

Dad: It's hard to think of another chemistry joke.

All the good ones Argon.

Dad: What do you do with chemicals when they die?

You Barium.

Dad: I have this extra electron I don't want.

My friend said, "Stop being so negative."

Dad: My nickname was bubbles in high school.

I always rose to the top.

Dad: Why did the cyclops stop teaching?

He only had one pupil.

Dad: Life without geometry...

is pointless.

Dad: I'm reading a book about anti-gravity.

It's impossible to put down.

Dad: Do you want to hear a joke about a piece of paper?

Never mind. It's tearable.

DAD THE IT GUY

Dad: Whenever I need to be refreshed after a long day,

I enjoy pressing the F5 key on my keyboard.

Dad: I lost control today.

Now I need to buy a new keyboard.

Dad: I love licking my F1 key.

I'm trying to get help.

Dad: My computer sings.

It's a Dell.

Dad: I typically avoid conversations with robots.

They just drone on.

Dad: What's Forrest Gump's computer password?

1forrest1.

Dad: Why did the developer go broke?

Because he used up all his cache.

Dad: Have you heard of the new band 843MB?

They're good, but they haven't gotten a gig yet.

Dad: If a dog was computer literate,

would his bark be worse than his byte?

Son: Why is there music coming from the printer?

Dad: Because it's jammin'.

Dad: I needed eight characters for a password,

so I chose Snow White and the seven dwarves.

Dad: What do you get if you take your computer to an ice rink?

A slipped disk.

Dad: A random email address keeps sending me pictures of canned meat.

I hate spam.

DON'T ASK DAD

Cashier: Any condiments with that?

Dad: You do look very nice today.

Cashier: Would you like the milk in the bag?

Dad: No, just keep it in the carton, please.

Kid: Dad, are you alright?

Dad: No, I'm half left.

Mom: How do I look?

Dad: With your eyes.

Kid: How does the turkey smell?

Dad: Probably with its beak.

Waitress: Do you want soup or salad?

Dad: No super salad for me. I'll just take a regular salad, please.

Kid: Dad, can you please make me a snack?

Dad: Poof! You're a snack.

Kid: Dad, I'm hungry.

Dad: Hi, Hungry, I'm Dad.

Kid: Dad, I'm serious!

Dad: I thought you said your name was Hungry.

Kid: Dad, did you put the cat out?

Dad: I didn't know it was on fire.

Kid: Dad, can you please put my shoes on?

Dad: I could, but I don't think they'll fit me very well.

Kid: Did you get a haircut?

Dad: No, I got them all cut.

Kid: Dad, can I watch the TV?

Dad: Sure, but don't turn it on.

Kid: How can you tell if an ant is a girl or a boy?

Dad: They're all girls otherwise they'd be uncles.

Kid: Can I call you later?

Dad: No, please call me Dad.

Kid: I think there's something in my shoe.

Dad: I'm pretty sure it's a foot.

Dad: Can I borrow an extension cord?
Kid: How long?

Dad: All day if you can spare it.

Kid: Where are my sunglasses?

Dad: I don't know. Where are my dad glasses?

Kid: Is this pool safe for diving?

Dad: It deep ends.

Waitress: Do you have reservations?

Dad: No, I'm confident I want to eat here.

Son: How many sheep do we have?

Dad: 48.

Son: We should round them up.

Dad: 50.

Kid: Do you know any jokes about sodium?

Dad: Na.

Kid: Can I set up Instagram on my phone?

Dad: Well, I don't know why you need Grandma on speed dial, but sure.

Kid: Dad, can I go in the bouncy castle?

Dad: It costs twice as much this year. That's inflation for you.

Doctor: Did you know you were color blind?

Dad: Well, that certainly came out of the purple.

Kid: I broke a guitar string last night.

Dad: Don't fret, I have another.

Kid: I was thinking about moving to Moscow.

Dad: *There's no need to be Russian into things.*

Kid: Why do you tell so many elevator jokes?

Dad: *Because they work on so many levels.*

Dad: I used to suffer from short stories.

Kid: Really? When?

Dad: *Once upon a time.*

Dad: What's the difference between a piano, a tuna, and glue?

You can't tuna fish, but you can tune a piano.

Kid: What about the glue?

Dad: I knew you'd get stuck on that.

CRAZY ABOUT CARS

A snail was really tired of being slow, so he went to the nearest Renault dealer and bought a car. He had them paint a big red S on the side (for "Snail"), so when everyone sees him, they will marvel at his new, speedier lifestyle, and exclaim,

"Wow! Look at that S-car-go!"

I told my Dad there was an accident today involving a van carrying a load of silverware.

He said I could find the accident site if I just looked for...

the fork in the road.

A man walks into an auto parts store and says to the mechanic,

"I'd like a set of wiper blades for my Yugo."

The mechanic thinks for a minute, then replies,

"OK. That sounds like a fair trade to me."

A young boy looking for some money went up to a man's door and asked him if he had any odd jobs. The man said, "I'll give you $50 to paint the porch out back."

The boy goes to work and after thirty minutes he comes back and tells the man he is done.

"Wow, that was fast," the man says.

The boy replied, "Yes, I know. But that wasn't a porch.

It was a Ferrari."

Dad: Where do Volkswagens go when they get old?

The Old Volks home.

Dad: What has four wheels and flies?

A garbage truck.